OFOTI

Other books by John Wheatcroft

Death of a Clown, poems, 1964
Prodigal Son, poems, 1967

OFOTI

by John Wheatcroft

SOUTH BRUNSWICK AND NEW YORK: A. S. BARNES AND COMPANY
LONDON: THOMAS YOSELOFF LTD

© 1970 by A. S. Barnes and Co., Inc.
Library of Congress Catalogue Card Number: 70-111788

A. S. Barnes and Co., Inc.
Cranbury, New Jersey 08512

Thomas Yoseloff Ltd
108 New Bond Street
London W1Y OQX, England

ISBN 0 498 07680 6
Printed in the United States of America

To Rachel, David and Allen

ACKNOWLEDGMENTS

Alcoa Playwriting Award, 1965

Produced for television by the

American Conservatory Theatre and WQED-TV

NET Playhouse, 1966–1969

National Educational Television Award, 1966

OFOTI

CHARACTERS

NARRATOR, A FAIRY
BOY
BOY'S MOTHER
RICH MAN'S CHAUFFEUR
RICH MAN'S SECRETARY
RICH MAN
WISE MAN
MARS MAN
HARLEQUIN
OFOTI, A TROLL
SOCRATES, A TURTLE
KALOTTÉ, A MERMAID
WISE MAN'S CHAUFFEUR
WISE MAN'S SECRETARY

ACT I

(*The stage is dark except for a spot of light on a Fairy, without wings, in a crimson gown, with loose black hair that hangs to her waist. She is standing stage right on the apron. As she reads from a large volume held flat in the palms of her hands, the curtain rises and a Boy sitting in bed reading a book is gradually lighted left. The Boy is dressed in a pair of red ski pajamas. The bed is merely two goal posts and a plank mattress. To the left of the bed is a stick window frame.*)

NARRATOR

Once there was a Boy who read a story about a troll. Now the troll in this story lived underneath a bridge, and whenever a passerby came walking across that bridge, the troll would eat him up. The Boy believed that eating people was not polite. And the idea of being eaten by a troll was frightening. For some reason the Boy always thought about being eaten by a troll just as it was time for him to go to sleep. It didn't help in the least for his mother to tell him that there really were no such beings as trolls anywhere on earth. (*Mother enters left, crosses to window, pantomimes pulling down shade, then kisses Boy goodnight. Silhouette effect. Mother exits left.*) Sometimes, when it lightninged (*Light flashes.*), he could see the fire of that troll's eye flash through the crack of his windowshade. And when it thundered

(Voices offstage boom like thunder. Offstage stamping of feet) he could hear that troll stamp his feet and growl. And sometimes, when the wind rushed through the leaves of the hickory tree in the yard beside his bedroom window *(Voices offstage huff like the wind.)*, the Boy could feel the breath of that troll as he came nearer and nearer. Then he would pull the covers up over his head *(Boy pantomimes.)* and his hair would stand up straight as a porcupine's. Well, one night *(Boy throws off covers and sits straight up in bed.)*, a very still night in spring—no lightning or thunder, not even a breeze tickling the leaves of the hickory tree, the moon so bright *(Light comes up green as Boy tiptoes across to window.)* it seemed like day outside, though maybe a little bit green—the Boy said to himself:

BOY

If my Mother's right and there are no such things as trolls on earth, then there's nothing to eat me up. Who's afraid of being eaten by nothing?

NARRATOR

So the Boy decided that the only thing to do was to find out once and for all about the realness of trolls. Deep in his heart he hoped that such a being as a troll really did exist, because, except for the impoliteness of eating people, he liked the whole idea of trolls really existing. And there was something about the sound of the word

BOY

Troll, troll, troll

NARRATOR

a soft, lovely, rolling sound, that pleased the Boy immensely. So, very quietly, he climbed through his window, slid down the rainspout *(Boy pantomimes raising shade, lifting window-sash, climbing through, sliding down spout, landing lightly on toes.)*, and landed softly on the grass underneath the hickory tree. He tiptoed across the yard, took one peek through the parlor window at his father and mother—whom he really did love, even though they never seemed to be interested in important or exciting things—and waving a good-bye that they could not see, started down the road. *(Boy pantomimes these things, using same window.)* Well, the Boy walked until he came to a creek he knew about from boat sailing and, clambering down underneath the bridge, he looked on this side and on that side, up near the road and down near the water. Then he shouted

BOY

Troll, troll, troll

NARRATOR

but in the green darkness he saw no creature and heard only the echo of his own voice.

(Offstage echo: Troll, troll, troll)

NARRATOR

So the Boy walked on until he came to another bridge, spanning a stream he had never seen before, and then a great big bridge over a wide, wide river. But although he searched and shouted, shouted and searched, he could not find a single troll. As the Boy went on walking—slowly now, for he was tired and, to tell the truth, a little bit discouraged—he suddenly saw a very curious automobile coming toward him.

(Headlights shine on stage from right.

Light off Narrator, who then exits. Upstage is darkened, and bed and window are removed. Limousine enters apron from right. It is merely a wooden frame with a steering wheel on a broomstick up front and with orange-crate seats front and back. Chauffeur, uniformed in purple and gold, and wearing heavy tortoiseshell glasses, powers by moving his feet. As he does so he makes sound of engine by fluttering his lips. Rising from back of front seat and from in between two rear seats, on which Secretary and Rich Man sit back to back,

[13]

*are telegraph poles to which are attached three wall-style tele-
phones with bells. A shorter telegraph pole with a telephone
on it rises behind the Chauffeur. Limousine is very long, about
three-quarters the length of the stage. When it stops in front
of Boy, about one-third from stage right, only Chauffeur
and wooden frame in the middle are on stage. Boy stands in
front of limousine and waves hand to stop it. Chauffeur stops
limousine, ceases to make noise of engine, picks up telephone
behind him and cranks bell.)*

CHAUFFEUR

Begging your pardon, sir—a boy is standing directly in front
of the limousine, waving his hand. Shall I run him down
or wait until he removes himself?

SECRETARY *(Offstage)*

Is he a sturdy-looking boy?

CHAUFFEUR

(Looking boy up and down) Why, I'd say so, sir.

SECRETARY

Hmmmmm. Wait until he gets out of our way. We want no
more repair bills.

CHAUFFEUR

Yes, sir. *(Hangs up telephone)*
(Boy walks around hood to where Chauffeur sits.)

BOY

Hello.

CHAUFFEUR

(Picking up and ringing telephone)
The Boy has said hello. Shall I answer him?

SECRETARY

By no means. Drive us up to him.

*(Chauffeur hangs up receiver, then starts motor and walks
limousine across apron. Secretary and Rich Man sitting in*

[14]

the rear of the limousine appear from right as Chauffeur disappears left. Secretary is dressed in tuxedo and wears derby. Rich Man is dressed in tails. High silk hat hangs from telegraph pole above telephones. Rich Man has shiny bald head. Both Secretary and Rich Man wear heavy tortoiseshell glasses. Secretary is studying a large map. Rich Man is playing a hard game of tiddleywinks with silver dollars on the orange-crate seat.)

BOY
(To Secretary)

Hello.

SECRETARY
(Not looking up from map)
Before you may speak to us you must secure an appointment. Is it a matter of importance?

BOY
Oh yes, very important.

SECRETARY
Well then, you may try to make an appointment.

BOY
Thank you, sir. But you see, I don't know how to make an appointment. I've never had to before.

SECRETARY
All you do is tell us when you want to speak to us. *(Putting down map and leafing through a huge black appointment book which he produces from under orange-crate seat)* Hmmmmmm. We have a minute and a half open next Thursday at 1:47 P.M., and three minutes on Monday the fourteenth—that's a week from this coming Friday—at 8:32 A.M. Unless you want to wait until sometime early next month.

BOY
Oh no, I couldn't do that. I couldn't even wait until tomorrow. You see, I want to talk to you right now.

Impossible. Those are the only appointments we have open. Personally we'd advise you to grab that Monday the fourteenth at 8:32. You have a full three minutes then. Otherwise, we're sorry.

BOY

Well, I guess I'll just have to go on looking. You see, I wanted to ask you if you'd ever come across a bridge that has a troll living underneath it.

SECRETARY

Too bad, too bad. If you only had an appointment you would be able to ask us. Of course, it wouldn't do you much good because we never have seen or heard of such a bridge anywhere. As a matter of fact, we're in the bridge business. Right now we own approximately half of all the bridges in the world and we're busy buying up the other half. Do you see this map? Well, every single known bridge in the whole world is right here and we can tell you not one of them has a troll living underneath it. So if we were you, Boy, we'd forget about that troll and . . .

(While Boy is staring at the map, a silver dollar from Rich Man's tiddleywink game arches high out of the back of the limousine. Boy catches it and tries to return it to Rich Man. Secretary intercepts by snatching it from Boy.)

SECRETARY

No, no, no. You mustn't. *(Secretary huffs on coin, polishes it on his sleeve, then obsequiously hands it to Rich Man.)*

RICH MAN

(Ringing Secretary on telephone. Secretary picks up telephone receiver. Rich Man and Secretary carry on conversation via telephone.) Ah, thank you, Thistlethwaite. See to it that that boy is given a reward. Anything he wants, mind you,

anything at all. And inform him that we like, no, we love people, especially boys.

BOY

Oh, thank you, sir. The only thing I want is a . . .

RICH MAN

Uh, uh, uh, my boy, not to me—to the Secretary. Always remember to work through the Secretary. (*Recommences tiddleywinks*) Thistlethwaite, see that this boy gets his . . . what did he say he wanted?

BOY

A troll, sir.

RICH MAN

No, no, no. Not to me. To him. Then he'll tell me. Always work through the Secretary. Believe me, boys who refuse to work through the Secretary come to bad ends.

BOY

I'm sorry sir. (*To Secretary*) I want a troll.

SECRETARY

Not yet, Boy. We still haven't asked you.

BOY

Oh, I'm awfully sorry.

SECRETARY

Well then, what is it you said you wanted, Boy?

BOY

A troll, sir, I want a troll.

SECRETARY

The Boy says he wants a troll, sir.

RICH MAN

Fine, fine. See that he is given a troll, Thistlethwaite, right away.

[17]

SECRETARY

Yes, sir. But we don't believe that we have a troll.

RICH MAN

Then get one. That's what I pay you for—to get what we don't already have. Call Farthington, Farthington, Farthington, and Lump and have them locate a troll and quote you a price.

SECRETARY

Yes, sir. *(Picks up third telephone, keeping his line to Rich Man in his other hand)* Operator, connect us with Farthington, Farthington, Farthington, and Lump . . . Hello, J. C. Farthington? . . . oh . . . B. L. Farthington? . . . oh . . . P. K. Farthington? . . . oh . . . Yes, we suppose we'll have to. Why must it always be him? . . . Hello, Lump? . . . This is Thistlethwaite, calling for Consolidated Enterprises Company Incorporated Limited. We are after a particular item, Lump . . . You will? . . . Fine . . . A troll . . . t-r-o-l-l . . . That's just what we said, a troll . . . Well, have you looked in the market index? . . . All right, but hurry it up. *(To Rich Man on other telephone)* We're sorry, sir, Lump is having difficulty locating one. But we're certain he'll manage to get his hands on a troll if there is any such item in any market on earth. You can count on Lump to . . . Excuse us, sir. *(On third telephone)* Hello . . . Yes . . . What? . . . Not a single one? . . . You did, eh. Well, Lump, we can't help feeling you've let us down . . . We're sorry, too, Lump. And we make no promises . . . Our future relations with you depend upon your ability to produce. Remember, there's always Geltch, Geltch, Geltch, and Hassenplug. Good-bye. *(To Rich Man)* We're terribly sorry, sir, to have to report that Lump has been unable to locate a single troll. There hasn't been one on the market for at least a hundred and fifty years. All of which forces us to conclude that there can be no such thing as a troll on the face of the earth.

RICH MAN

Quite right, Thistlethwaite, quite right. Apparently the troll, whatever *it* was, simply proved to be of no use in the modern world. Tell the Boy I'm sorry, but I wouldn't want to give him something that was of no use anyhow. Tell him to ask for something else. You might suggest a bridge. We have practically cornered the bridge market, you know, and can easily spare one.

SECRETARY

Yes, sir. *(To Boy)* We're awfully sorry, Boy, but we cannot provide you with a troll. And you wouldn't want to own something which is of no use anyhow. So . . .

BOY

Oh, yes, I would, sir. I don't care how useless a troll is. A troll is just what I want.

SECRETARY

So why don't you ask for something else? A bridge, say. To own a piece of property is the most fortunate thing that can happen to any boy.

BOY

But I don't want to own a bridge unless there's a troll living underneath it.

SECRETARY *(To Rich Man)*

We're sorry to have to interrupt you again, sir, but the Boy will not take a bridge without a troll.

RICH MAN

What? Will not take a bridge?

SECRETARY

A very headstrong boy. Frankly, sir, we recommend that we wash our hands of him.

RICH MAN

Quite right, Thistlethwaite, quite right. A boy who shows no interest in owning a bridge has no promise. Instruct the

[19]

chauffeur to drive on. (*Lowers voice*) Remember, we must locate that bridge where the rainbow ends and the pot of gold is buried, if you know what I mean. (*Raises voice*) Inform the Boy that if he should ever change his mind and should decide to make something of himself in life, he need only let us know and he shall have his bridge.

SECRETARY

Yes, sir. (*To Boy*) If you ever change your mind, Boy, and get some sense, let us know and we'll see that you are given a bridge to begin to make your fortune with.

BOY

Thank you very much, sir, and thank him too. But I'm sure I'll never want a bridge unless it has a troll living underneath it.

SECRETARY

Our frank advice to you, Boy, is that you get your feet on the ground (*Lifts feet from stage to frame of automobile as he half falls down*) and your hands on some property. (*Secretary's hands clutch air. On telephone to Chauffeur*) Drive on. Keep your eyes open for any bridges we do not own (*Drops voice*), especially the bridge at the end of the rainbow.

CHAUFFEUR (*Offstage*)

Yes, sir.

(*Chauffeur makes engine noise and walks limousine off-stage. Boy watches it go, then hangs head and walks slowly on, downstage right.*)

BOY

Although the Rich Man may be right and there may be no such being on earth as a troll, I'll go on searching.

(*Inclined plank, representing a hill, is slid onto apron from right. As Boy starts to plod up plank, Wise Man with wheel-barrow comes zig-zagging down. Wise Man has dark tortoise-shell glasses without lenses. His dusty, frayed coat is mis-*

[20]

buttoned. A notebook with a huge pencil dangling from it on a string sticks out of his pocket. His white hair is wild and long. He has a very red face with a large red nose. The wheelbarrow is overloaded with encyclopedic volumes. On the back edge of the wheelbarrow there is a lectern with a book open and a little light over the book, from which the Wise Man is reading, pronouncing gibberish to himself, as he comes on. As Boy tries to avoid wheelbarrow to the right, it veers toward him. Then to the left, then back to the right, where Boy and wheelbarrow collide, spilling books, knocking over Boy and Wise Man. Boy immediately begins collecting books and placing them carefully back in the wheelbarrow. Wise Man loses glasses and sits sprawled. He howls.)

WISE MAN

Why don't you look where I'm going?

(Wise Man gropes for glasses, gets his hands on a book and tries to place it on his nose. Boy spies glasses and fits them on Wise Man. Wise Man then frantically begins to collect books, hugging them to himself.)

WISE MAN

A fine thing to scatter a man's glasses, send his books flying off his nose *(Trying to find book he had been reading)* and make him lose his road.

BOY

I'm awfully sorry, sir.

WISE MAN

Sorry? Every fool's sorry after the damage is done. But who's going to find my place in this wheelbarrow again, eh? *(Boy helps Wise Man to his feet and steadies him.)* Well, what have you to say for yourself?

BOY

I . . . I . . . I tried . . .

WISE MAN

Nothing. Just as I thought. Nothing. *(Lifts spectacles and looks at Boy)* And only a boy, too. Why aren't you in school, Boy?

BOY

Why, because it's nighttime, sir. I only go to school during the day.

WISE MAN

A very poor excuse. Can't you see that if you had been in school you would never have knocked over my portable library?

BOY

No, sir . . . I mean, yes, sir.

WISE MAN

There you are—proved by your own admission. A foolproof argument. Excuse me a minute, Boy, while I write that down. *(Fumbles in pockets for notebook)* You see, I keep bumping into people all the time . . . I mean people keep bumping into me. So if I just had that argument . . . *(Search becomes frantic.)*

BOY

Is this what you're looking for, sir? *(Boy hands Wise Man notebook with pencil hanging from it on string attached to top pocket of Wise Man's coat.)*

WISE MAN

Ah, yes, my boy . . . Thank you. *(Opens notebook)* Now, I'll just write that down. *(Ready to write)* Dear me, I seem not to have a pencil. *(Begins frantically to search Boy for pencil)* I know I put it in one of these pockets.

BOY

Excuse me, sir, but that's my pocket you're looking in, not yours.

WISE MAN
(Examines cloth close to his eyes)
Why, so it is. How in the world did your pocket get on me?

BOY
It didn't, sir. My pocket's on me. That's your pocket on you.

WISE MAN
(Tugs Boy's pajamas and Boy bumps into him)
So it is. Goodness, you're a clever boy. *(Searches his own coat pockets)*

BOY
Excuse me again, sir, but is this what you're looking for?
(Holds up pencil)

WISE MAN
Ah, to be sure. I haven't run into a boy as smart as you in many a day. Now let me see. *(Scratches head, stares into air, sucks on pencil, hums, walks up and down with hands behind back, sucks pencil again)* Oh, I've gone and forgotten it. A brilliant idea lost to mankind forever. Oh, dear me.

BOY
I beg your pardon, sir, but I can remember it. You said, "If you had been in school, you would never have knocked over my portable library. A foolproof argument."

WISE MAN
(Has been writing furiously)
Bless you, my boy, you're right. *(Looks at what he has written from a distance, with pride)* I can see that you've a head on your shoulders. You have a magnificent future ahead of you. *(Shakes hands)* And in return for the great kindness you have just done me, you may ask me any question you like about anything on earth. You see, my boy, I'm the wisest man in the whole world. These books with all of their wisdom—mine, all mine.

BOY

Gosh!

WISE MAN

So think hard, Boy.

BOY

Oh, I don't have to think at all, sir. I know what I want to know.

WISE MAN

Don't be hasty . . . or foolish . . . remember, just one question. That's all I can spare the time for. (*Whispers*) I'm at work on a very important project.

BOY

Oh, sir, I'm so happy I've found someone who can answer my question.

WISE MAN

Yes, indeed. You are a most fortunate boy. Not every young wheelbarrow I run into . . . I mean, not every young wheelbarrow that runs into me . . . I mean, not every young man I stumble . . . I mean, not every young man that stumbles me . . . that is . . . for goodness sake, Boy, aren't you ready with that question yet?

BOY

I've been ready a long time, sir. All I want to know is, where in the world can I find a troll?

WISE MAN

. . . find a troll . . . in the world . . . where . . . A good question. An excellent question. You are a clever fellow, aren't you?

BOY

Thank you, sir.

WISE MAN

Don't thank me, my boy. You deserve at least part of the

credit. Now let's shake hands before we go. (*Pumps Boy's hand, then seizes shafts of wheelbarrow*)

BOY

But sir, you haven't answered my question.

WISE MAN

Oh, dear me. Did I neglect to answer your question? (*Whispers*) You see, my boy, I've got so much on my mind that's so very important . . . The answer is simple. All you have to do is look under the proper classification in the proper book. Hmm . . . (*Strokes chin*) "Troll." Of course. "Protoactinium." (*Roots through books, seizes a volume at random, runs finger up and down three or four pages, slowly closes book*) What was that again, Boy?

BOY

A troll, sir.

WISE MAN

Ah, yes. A troll. (*Scratches head*) Certainly, certainly. "Prothalamion." (*Pulls nose*) Hmm. A troll, you say?

BOY

Yes sir, a troll.

WISE MAN

"Protochordate," "prototrophic," "protractor" . . . (*Pages furiously as he pronounces these words, then suddenly stops finger and reads to himself*)

BOY

"Protractor"? Why, you can't find out anything about a troll by looking under "protractor." A protractor is used to measure angles. Everybody knows that. Why don't you look under "troll"?

WISE MAN

Under "troll"—of course! You are a bright young fellow. (*Dives for book, turns pages furiously, then slows down*)

Troll . . . trrroooollll. What did you say the first letter of troll is?

BOY

Why, it's t—troll, t-r-o-l-l. Everybody knows how to spell troll.

WISE MAN

To be sure, t-r-o-l-l. *(Thumbing slowly)* Ah, here it is. "Troll." See what you can do, my boy, when you know how to use your tools?

BOY

I'm so glad, I'm so glad. Quickly, tell me what it says.

WISE MAN

Troll. A mythical bear-like monster said to inhabit inland waters.

BOY

Go on, go on.

WISE MAN

That's all.

BOY

That's all? But it doesn't answer my question. I want to know where on earth I can find a troll who lives underneath a bridge.

WISE MAN

Why, the answer is as plain as my nose on your face . . . I mean, your face on my nose . . . I mean, my face on your nose . . . I mean, your nose on my face . . . Trolls are mythical, which means not real, and they inhabit water, which is not earth. So, it must be perfectly clear, even to a silly boy like you, that trolls do not exist anywhere in the world. Can you see now why it pays to be wise? My advice to you, Boy, is that you plant your feet on the ground. *(Takes a firm stand in front of wheelbarrow)* Forget about all these mythical ideas of yours, which are only going to lead you

[26]

into trouble. *(Starts to walk and bumps into wheelbarrow)* Get yourself something you can put your hands on, like a portable library *(Grabs shafts of wheelbarrow)*, and keep knowledge at your fingertips *(Reaches toward books with one hand so that wheelbarrow would fall over if Boy did not save it)*, and then you'll be moving in the right direction. *(Strains to move wheelbarrow backward up inclined plane, but feet seem fastened to the stage)* Would you mind giving me a little push to get me started on my way again, my boy? *(Boy pushes Wise Man and Wise Man stumbles up hill backwards, veering to right and left. Shouts back at Boy)* Take my advice, if you want to turn into something! *(Crashes into large rock at top and falls with wheelbarrow over edge of incline)*

(Boy sits dejectedly down on rock, on apron at bottom of incline, chin in hands.)

BOY

I guess the Wise Man must be right. I guess the only real things are the things you see every day—rich men and secretaries and chauffeurs and automobiles and wise men and wheelbarrows and books. Perhaps even the moon isn't real or the stars or the rainbow, because they're not really anywhere on Earth. And yet *(Looks up)* I can see them. There's the moon and there are the stars and there's . . .

(Flash of multi-colored light. Mars Man makes a gentle swooooosh as he descends to center stage just behind proscenium in a trash can. Mars Man has long blond hair and a long full blond beard. He wears only a pair of bathing trunks. His body and trunks are painted gold. He stands very straight with arms folded across his chest. Boy leaps from rock and rubs his eyes.)

MARS MAN
(Stepping out of trash can onto apron)

Hello, Earth Boy.

BOY

Why—hello. Where did you come from?

MARS MAN

From Mars, where I live.

BOY

But how did you get here—on Earth—from Mars?

MARS MAN

Didn't you see me arrive? I came in my imagination ship.

BOY

You couldn't come down from Mars in that. It's nothing but a trash can. It doesn't even have a rocket engine.

MARS MAN

It doesn't need a rocket engine. Everyone in the universe but Earth men have always known that imagination can take you any place you want to go. All you do is start to imagine and say swooooosh.

BOY

Why, that's perfectly marvelous! But tell me, Mr. Mars Man, do Space beings use the same language as we do on Earth?

MARS MAN

Goodness no. No one from Space ever breaks the Lovely Silence of the universe. Instead of talking, we think to each other and we think answers to each other's thoughts. "Thought-uage" is what you would have to call it in Earth language.

BOY

"Thoughtuage"? That's a funny word. "Thoughtuage" . . .

MARS MAN

It certainly is a funny word. But, you see, it's not really a word at all. It's communion.

[28]

Gosh. But how is it, Mr. Mars Man, that you can speak Earth language, if you only use thoughtuage in space?

MARS MAN

Well, it's this way. We Space beings have what you might call wireless telephones built right into our ears. We can hear any noise made in the Lovely Silence of the universe from any place all the time, including Earth language. In fact, our problem is to keep from hearing, because there's so much ugly sound coming from your planet. That's why for years now I've tried to listen to just the sweetness of children's voices, especially yours.

BOY

Gosh. And can you really hear something now, when everything seems silent to me?

MARS MAN (*Shaking head*)

I hear all kinds of noises. The closest is an ugly voice speaking foolish words. It's saying, "What do you mean by bumping into me that way? I'm the wisest man in the world." (*Claps hands over ears*) Oh, I can't stand any more of that! (*Takes hands off*) And now I hear an engine of some sort, going rrrrrr, and bells ringing, and a voice saying, "Tell her I like, no, love people, especially little girls." And now another voice saying, "Yes, sir. And remember, we like, no, love, people, especially little girls." (*Claps hands over ears again*) Oh, I can't stand that either. Will you please start talking to me, Earth Boy, so that I can take my ears off such ugly sounds and foolish words?

BOY

I'll be glad to, Mr. Mars Man. In fact, there's a question I'd like to ask you. It's about Space. You see, I've never been there or even met any one before who has.

[29]

MARS MAN

I'll be glad to answer your question if I can.

BOY

Well, the reason I've come walking down this road tonight is that I'm searching for a troll who lives underneath a bridge and eats people up. A rich man I met told me that there is no such thing as a troll in the whole world and a wise man told me there is no such thing as a troll anywhere on Earth and my mother told me that trolls are just imaginary. Do you know where in Space there might be a troll, Mr. Mars Man?

MARS MAN

A troll? . . . No, I'm awfully sorry but I've never come across a troll anywhere in the Lovely Silence. Of course, I haven't been everywhere and I don't know about every being. And I promise I'll keep a thought out. But I must say, I have my doubts about there being such a thing as a troll anywhere in Space.

BOY

Oh.

MARS MAN

Well *(Looking at sky)*, I guess I'd better imagine myself back into Space. Seeing you sitting here all alone, I just decided I ought to drop down and make sure that everything was all right. For a long time now I've been wanting to hear you in person and to talk to you in Earth language. It's been very pleasant. *(Folding arms across chest)* Good luck in finding the troll.

BOY

Thank you, Mr. Mars Man.

MARS MAN

Good-bye, Earth Boy. If you ever need me for anything, just call. I'll be listening.

BOY

Good-bye, Mr. Mars Man.

MARS MAN

Swooooosh. (*Is raised in trash can*)

(*Boy watches Mars Man go. At first he waves brightly,
then more and more faintly. Finally he stops with his hand
out in the air, motionless, then suddenly drops it.*

*Boy sits down on rock again, dejected, with chin in his
palms. A tear spills over the rim of his eye and he rubs it
from his cheek with the back of his hand. He looks off into
space in direction of Mars Man's departure.*

*Out from behind rock pops Harlequin. He wears an artist's
beret and smock. Smock is ragged, as are pants, and shoes
are oversized with toes sticking out. There is a bell on his
beret and there are bells on his sleeves and shoes. They jingle
as he moves. He carries a huge paintbrush, much as a jester
carries a stick. Although he is slightly stooped, he moves
lightly and quickly.*

*Harlequin stands in front of Boy to left, looking at him
with his head cocked. Boy does not see Harlequin at first.
Harlequin sits down on rock beside Boy, and out of sympathy
falls into imitative mournfulness. Then Boy notices him but
pays almost no attention.*)

BOY (*To himself*)

Oh dear. I suppose it's all a waste of time. If the Rich Man
and the Wise Man are right about Earth and if the Mars Man
is right about Space, then there's no place left for a troll
to exist. I guess I'll just have to go back home and be afraid
again every night. I do wish there were such a being as a
troll, somewhere, so that once and for all I could see him.
I know I'd never be afraid again.

(*Harlequin has been listening attentively. Suddenly he leaps
from the rock, turns a somersault, and in pantomime urges*

[31]

Boy to follow him. Boy at first pays no attention, then watches, hesitates, follows as though reluctant. Harlequin keeps pointing ahead with his paint brush. He and Boy begin to run, hand in hand. Flat of tree stump house with door in it slides across stage from left toward Harlequin and Boy as they stop actual running and run in place. They allow the door of the flat to pass over them and then flat passes off stage right. At instant they pass through door, back stage is lighted and the interior of a tree stump house is revealed. In the center of the back wall there is a huge white television screen. Or maybe it's a picture window. The walls of tree stump house [flats] are large bright orange, red, green, purple murals of animals, harlequins, acrobats, children. Harlequin seats Boy on large paint can [in pantomime, of course] and breaks into a comic dance to the music of the "Troll Song," just in front of the television screen. Boy laughs despite himself. When Harlequin has finished, Boy applauds, then checks himself and looks sad. Harlequin again tries to make him laugh but Boy says)

BOY

Please don't make me laugh any more. I really think you're awfully funny. But right now I want to be sad. You see, it's because I can't find the troll.

(At the word "troll," Harlequin dips brush in an open paint can and begins to paint in purple with huge strokes on white paper screen a life-sized cartoon drawing of the troll. Boy sits with chin in hands, unaware of what Harlequin is doing. When Harlequin has finished drawing troll, he reaches over with paint brush and touches Boy, then directs Boy's attention to troll he has drawn, using brush as pointer.)

BOY

Oh, that's a lovely picture of a troll! It's exactly like the troll I'm looking for.

(In pantomime Harlequin tells Boy troll is his to keep.)

[32]

Ofoti, the modern fairy tale that concerns a boy's search for a Troll. Here are The Boy (John Tragard) and Ofoti the Troll (Rene Auberjonois) in a scene from the N.E.T. Playhouse production. (Courtesy WQED-Tv and N.E.T. Playhouse)

The Boy runs from the motorcycle people. (Courtesy WQED-Tv and N.E.T. Playhouse)

BOY

Thank you very much. But, you see, that troll is—well, he's just painted on a piece of paper, and the troll I'm trying to find lives underneath a bridge.

(Harlequin signals wait, turns, and draws a cartoon bridge over troll.)

BOY

That's a very nice bridge, and you're really very kind to draw it for me. But it's still not a real troll, you know.

(Harlequin suddenly stands very still and straight. He closes his eyes, lifts up his head, and crosses his arms on his chest. Slowly he turns his face toward the troll and opens his eyes and gradually smiles. Boy rises to his feet in expectation. Smile on Harlequin's face is agony and joy. Loud cymbal crash offstage as Ofoti the Troll leaps through screen exactly where Harlequin has drawn him.

Ofoti is a man who looks something like a bear. No attempt to make him look non-human. Wears brown gloves and brown tights and brown turtleneck sweater. Has a great deal of brown hair on head and a short-cropped brown beard and mustache. Pointed ears show through hair. He lands on toes, staring at Boy, who jumps back in fear and surprise. Harlequin's smile becomes sweet. All three hold poses.)

CURTAIN

ACT II

(As the curtain rises, stage lights gradually. Boy and Ofoti are in frozen positions. Rock bridge arches overhead and to the left. To the right there is a door with a huge rock outside, visible. Across the back of the stage can be seen the interior of the tree stump house with the broken paper screen. Boy and Ofoti come to life. Ofoti goes into fierce song and dance. Boy cowers, then checks himself and stands. During first part of song and dance Ofoti snaps at Boy as though to eat him. Boy almost runs in terror but doesn't. Ofoti gradually becomes less and less fierce, then less and less vigorous until finally he sits down cross-legged in center of apron. Boy slowly edges closer. Ofoti becomes gentle, then pathetic, and ends song crying. Boy is melted and tries to comfort him.)

TROLL SONG

A troll is a terrible, terrible thing
With a hideous, horrible sting;
    How he enjoys
    To gnaw on boys:
A creature bold—that's a troll!

A troll is a cold-hearted, hard-hearted beast
With an earth-shaking, breath-taking squeeze;
    His great delight,
    To cause boys fright:
A heart that's cold—that's a troll!

A troll's an unfortunate sort of a chap,
There's no place for his bridge on the map;
    No boy that breathes,
    In him believes:
Hapless and old—that's a troll!

A troll is a creature without any worth,
He's the loneliest being on earth;
    No boy would cry
    If he should die:
Unwanted soul—that's a troll!

BOY

Don't cry, Mr. Troll. I'm a boy and I believe in you. And
if you should die, I'd cry.

OFOTI

Do you really care that I'm unhappy?

BOY

Oh, yes, Mr. Troll.

OFOTI

Please don't go on calling me "Mr. Troll."

BOY

What else can I call you?

OFOTI

If you won't laugh, I'll tell you what my name is.

BOY

Oh, I wouldn't think of laughing. I promise.

[35]

OFOTI

Well . . . it's . . . well . . . it's Ofoti.

BOY

Ofoti? Ofoti. What a lovely sound! I think it's the most beautiful name I've ever heard. Ō-fō-ti.

OFOTI

Why, you don't seem at all like a human being. Even your voice is soft. Most humans have such ugly voices and make so much noise all the time. That's why trolls have always lived under bridges or down under the water—to get away from the sound of people.

BOY

I never realized that before.

OFOTI

But that's not the worst of it. Human beings are awfully cruel. Why, one of my great uncles, Uncle Fenrir, was killed by a goat owned by a human being. Would you believe it, the man's goat butted my Uncle Fenrir right off the very bridge he lived under?

BOY

I read all about that in a book. But I don't think your Uncle Fenrir was a very well-mannered troll, Ofoti. Every time someone tried to pass across the bridge, he'd eat them up.

OFOTI

Oh, what a terrible thing to say! It's just what humans have always said. But there's not a word of truth in it. No troll ever ate a human being. Look at me. Do I look as though I'd eat you up?

BOY

Well, no. I can see you're a very gentle troll.

OFOTI

That's kind of you to say. I'm sorry I got so angry and hurt, because really I owe you a great deal. You see, while most human beings have been killing trolls right and left for centuries, you've just saved my life.

BOY

Saved your life? How?

OFOTI

Well, it's a funny thing, and how it came about I certainly don't know. Not even my grandfather could explain it. But unless some human being lets a troll know that he believes in him at least once every hundred years, the troll will die. It's been just ninety-nine years three hundred and sixty-four days since the last person saw me. I had less than a day to live. If you hadn't come along when you did, I'd surely have died of neglect, knowing that I was no longer believed in by any human being. How can I thank you enough!

(Ofoti impetuously runs toward Boy and grabs him to hug him. Boy cries out in terror and struggles to get away.)

BOY

Oh, help, help! The troll is after me! The troll is after me!

OFOTI

(Leaping back, with paws in the air, then hanging head, deeply hurt) There I knew it. *(Begins to cry softly)* I was trying to hug you and you thought I was going to . . . to . . .   *(Sobs)*

BOY

Oh, Mr. Troll . . . I mean, Ofoti. I've hurt your feelings again. Ofoti, dear Ofoti, please don't cry. It's because I was so frightened of trolls before I met you. You see, I never knew what a troll is really like. *(Solicitously comforts Ofoti)*

OFOTI

(Shrinking, but with pride) That's all right. It's not as if a troll doesn't have friends. There are very many other beings that like and understand trolls, you know.

[37]

I'm sure there are.

OFOTI

And . . . *(A knocking on rock)* Excuse me. There's someone knocking on my bridge. It's probably Socrates. I've been expecting him for the last fourteen or fifteen months. *(Boy rises to go.)* Oh, please don't go. *(Admitting Socrates)* Come in, Socrates. How are you this year?

(Socrates is a very wide turtle in a bright green shell with a flat white stomach. He walks upright. Except for his shell, there is no attempt to make him seem non-human. He takes very slow, heavy, short steps.)

SOCRATES

Ah, good to see you, Ofoti. I just thought I'd . . . *(Sees Boy, stops, then retreats a little faster than he entered)* Well, I guess I'll be poking along. Maybe we can get together sometime the year after next. I . . . uh . . . I promised my cousin Alcibiades . . .

OFOTI

Wait a minute, Socrates. I mean wait a week or two. Please don't go. Really he's not like most human beings. In fact . . .

SOCRATES

I'm sure he's a perfectly fine human being, Ofoti, and every one is entitled to pick his own friends. But I must be lagging along.

OFOTI

Believe me, he has a very lovely voice. When he hurts your feelings he does it so beautifully and gently—without even meaning to. Besides, you know my hundred years was almost up . . .

SOCRATES

Not so soon again. Why it seems like just ten years ago that I heard from Kalotté the mermaid that . . .

OFOTI

It was up tomorrow, Socrates. And he saved my life. So won't you please stay—as a special favor to me?

SOCRATES

Believe me, Ofoti, I wouldn't do this for anyone but you.

OFOTI

Thank you, Socrates. Socrates, I want you to meet a human being.

BOY

How do you do, Socrates?

SOCRATES

How do you do, human being?

BOY

Why do turtles dislike people so much, Socrates? After all, human beings haven't treated you the way they—I mean, we—have trolls, have we? We all still believe in you.

SOCRATES

Turtles don't depend on your belief for their existence, the way trolls do. We have other complaints.

BOY

Tell me what they are. Maybe I can explain them to human beings and get them to stop.

SOCRATES

Oh, it's not so easy as that. Some of it—like painting our stomachs and putting us in goldfish bowls or like taking our shells and making frames for glasses out of them—well, those things you might get stopped, though I personally have my doubts.

BOY

Oh, those are terrible, terrible things!

[39]

SOCRATES

But the feeling human beings have had about us for hundreds and hundreds of years—*that* you can't do anything about. It's a perpetual wrong.

BOY

What feeling do you mean, Socrates?

SOCRATES

Why, you know as well as I do that human beings think that we turtles are the funniest and the stupidest of all creatures. Even when they claim to be saying something good about us, they're really slandering our character. Take that ridiculous story about the tortoise and the hare . . .

BOY

Oh, I read that story in school. The tortoise and the hare were having a race and . . .

SOCRATES

(Covering his ears with his hands) Please, please, I can't bear to listen to it.

BOY

But, Socrates, the tortoise finally wins the race.

SOCRATES

Precisely. All creatures except human beings hate races. We run only when we have to—to get away from people, for example. Come now, have you ever seen turtles or trolls or any other animals having a race?

BOY

Well, I . . . I guess I haven't, now that you mention it.

SOCRATES

You know you haven't! Nothing is so stupid as racing. And turtles especially hate to run. We pride ourselves on the slow dignity with which we move and on always having a specific purpose for going somewhere. And so to make up a ridiculous story about a turtle's having beaten a rabbit in a race . . . well, it's just too humiliating.

BOY

Gosh, Socrates, I never realized . . .

SOCRATES

Of course you never realized. That's exactly the trouble with men. They don't know how to realize.

BOY

Gosh! Would you mind if I asked you a few questions, Socrates, just so I can get some idea of how much a really wise being knows?

SOCRATES

Go right ahead, my boy.

BOY

Hmm . . . How much is 1739 times 9375 minus 2,928,125 divided by 2 million plus 2,673,178 minus 4,673,177?

SOCRATES

Ah, that's an easy one.

BOY

Well, then, what's the answer?

SOCRATES

Why, I've already told you.

BOY

No, you haven't.

SOCRATES

Of course, I have. Didn't you hear me say *one*, an easy *one*. *One* is the answer.

BOY

Gosh, I never realized that turtles are so smart. Why, you had the answer faster than a computer.

SOCRATES

I should hope so. Imagine, comparing the brain of a turtle with a machine. Why don't you ask me a hard question?

[41]

Well, I'll try. Hmm . . . hmm . . . hmm . . . Socrates, tell me, where did trolls come from? I mean, at the very beginning? Where did the first troll come from?

OFOTI

Why, that's a very interesting question, Socrates. I wonder why I never thought of asking it myself.

SOCRATES *(Hanging head)*

Oh my, how awful! I just don't know where in the world trolls do come from. What a humiliation! The first time in my life I've been asked a question I can't answer. By a human being! *(Socrates breaks into sobs. Boy and Ofoti run over to comfort him.)*

OFOTI

Don't feel bad, Socrates.

BOY

Please don't cry. Oh, it's all my fault! Why must I always be saying the wrong thing?

OFOTI

You see, Socrates, he really is a fine boy, isn't he?

SOCRATES

I don't blame him. It's just . . . not being able to answer a question thought up by a human being. I'll never take my head out of my shell again. *(Puts head in shell)* Oh no, I'll never look another turtle in the snapper. What a disgrace!

OFOTI

Don't cry, Socrates, please. We'll never breathe a word of it to anyone. *(Knock on rock)* Oh dear, excuse me, there's someone at my bridge.

(Ofoti admits Kalotté the Mermaid. Kalotté is dressed in a green sheath, with gold sequins, that tapers to a tail. She walks on her toes, like a toe dancer, taking very tiny steps.

Her golden hair hangs down to her ankles and whips and swishes as she turns. She carries a green mask on a stick, which she uses as a veil.)

OFOTI

Why, it's Kalotté the Mermaid! Come in, Kalotté, come in.
(Kalotté starts to enter, but sees Boy and stops dead. Quickly veils face)

KALOTTÉ

Oh! *(Soft scream)*

OFOTI

Don't be afraid, Kalotté. He won't hurt you.

KALOTTÉ
(Backing rapidly toward rock door)
But, but he's, he's . . . !

OFOTI

He's really very nice, though. And not at all noisy. Socrates felt the same way, but now he doesn't mind him very much, do you, Socrates?

SOCRATES

Well, not very much. *(Coming slowly out of shell)* How do you do, Kalotté?

KALOTTÉ

I'd be fine if it weren't for . . .

OFOTI

Maybe you'd forgotten, Kalotté, that tomorrow was to be my last day again. He saved my life. So please let me introduce you to each other.

KALOTTÉ

Well, if you're sure he won't pull my hair, Ofoti.

OFOTI

Human being, I'd like you to meet Kalotté the Mermaid.

[43]

She's the most beautiful creature in the whole world. (*Kalotté removes her veil.*)

BOY

Gosh, she is beautiful. How do you do?

OFOTI (*Whispers to Kalotté*)

Doesn't he have a gentle voice for a you-know-what?

KALOTTÉ (*To Ofoti*)

Yes, he really does. I'd hardly believe he was one if I weren't looking at him with my own eyes. (*To Boy*) How do you do?

BOY

Are you by any chance the Mermaid who lives underneath the rainbow?

KALOTTÉ (*In alarm*)

Why, yes. But how do you know?

BOY

Oh, I read all about you in a book. But I've never been able to hear your beautiful voice.

OFOTI

I'm sure Kalotté would be glad to sing for you, wouldn't you, Kalotté?

KALOTTÉ

If you'd really like me to.

BOY

Oh, please do.

MERMAID'S SONG

I am not a being human,
Animal or mineral;
And except for songs and dreams I
Never would have been-at-all.

[44]

I am not a Rich Man, Wise Man,
Not a Turtle, Boy, or Troll;
I am just a green-tailed Mermaid
And my hair is spun of gold.

And my home is not like humans',
Not a bridge, and not a tree;
I live underneath the rainbow
With the turtles in the sea.

There's a Troll whose name's Ofoti,
There's a Turtle, Socrates;
I am just a gold-haired Mermaid
And my name is Kalotté.

BOY *(Clapping)*

You do have the most beautiful voice I've ever heard, Kalotté.

SOCRATES

It's too bad some other people don't think so. The human being who pulled her hair, for instance.

BOY

What would make any human being pull Kalotté's hair?

SOCRATES

You tell him, Kalotté, it's your story.

KALOTTÉ

Well, to begin with, human beings don't believe in me. That's why they can't hear my songs.

BOY

Gosh, and are you going to die the way Ofoti was?

KALOTTÉ

Oh, no. You see, I can't die. Only trolls die if human beings don't believe in them. As long as there's a rainbow over the sea I'll go on living.

BOY

How lucky you are to live underneath the rainbow!

KALOTTÉ

Well, yes and no. You see, that's how I got my hair pulled.

BOY

Because you live underneath the rainbow?

KALOTTÉ

Exactly. One day a human being who was fishing near my home dipped his hand deep into the water, and shouting "Gold! Gold! I've found the pot of gold at the end of the rainbow!" pulled my hair up out of the sea. I almost died of fright.

BOY

What a terrible thing! Did he try to lift you into his boat or to cut off your hair?

KALOTTÉ

No, that wouldn't have been so bad. *(Ready to cry)* He just stared at my hair in his hands and then shouted in the ugliest voice you can imagine . . . *(Sobbing)* It makes me ill just to think of it. Oh, I can't say it.

SOCRATES

He shouted that Kalotté's beautiful golden hair was just worthless old seaweed.

OFOTI

Why, that human being had in his hands half of all the wealth in the world.

BOY

Gosh. But if Kalotté's hair is worth half the wealth in the world, I know who owns the other half.

ALL THREE

You do? Who?

Why, the Rich Man.

SOCRATES

Man, you say? I don't believe it.

BOY

Really, it's true. The Rich Man owns half the bridges in the world and he's going to buy all of the rest. Only a very rich man could do that.

SOCRATES

Pooh, bridges don't mean anything, except to trolls, and all they want is one to live under. But hair—that's a different matter. Ofoti told you the Mermaid's golden hair is worth half the wealth of the world. Well, there it is, right before your eyes. Look at it. *(Kalotté pirouettes, swinging her hair.)* Is it beautiful, or isn't it?

BOY

Oh, yes, it is beautiful. The most beautiful hair I've ever seen.

SOCRATES

I should think it is. Now feel it. *(Kalotté bends forward, throwing her hair up over her head so that it falls into the Boy's hands.)* Is it soft? Is it fine? Have you ever felt anything so precious?

BOY

No, I never have, Socrates.

SOCRATES

Now, suppose you tell us about the hair of this human who is supposed to have the other half of the wealth of the world.

BOY

Why . . . why . . . why . . . I . . .

SOCRATES

Go on, go on. What is his hair like?

BOY

It's . . . uh . . . that is . . .

SOCRATES

Is it gold?

BOY

No, it isn't gold.

SOCRATES

Not gold. Is it silver, then?

BOY

Oh . . . no, it isn't silver either.

SOCRATES

Is it as long as Kalotté's? Does it hang to his ankles?

BOY

No.

SOCRATES

To his waist?

BOY

No.

SOCRATES

Just how long is it then?

BOY

Well . . . it's . . . I must tell the truth. The Rich Man doesn't have any hair at all.

(Ofoti, Socrates, and Kalotté break into laughter.)

BOY

Well, I don't see what's so funny about that. And I don't think it's very polite to laugh at me—just because I'm a human being. I can't help it any more than you can help being lucky things like trolls and turtles and mermaids. I . . . I . . . I . . . I think you're as mean as . . . as . . . *(Sobs)*

(Kalotté and Ofoti run over to comfort Boy; Socrates lumbers toward him.)

[48]

OFOTI

There, there, don't cry, dear Boy.

SOCRATES

It's not your fault that you don't know anything about wealth.

KALOTTÉ

Please, don't cry. Because I have a wonderful idea—something that will make us all happy, the happiest beings on earth.

ALL THREE

What is it? Tell us, tell us.

KALOTTÉ

Well, the reason I came to see you today, Ofoti, is that I want to invite you to a party at my house in the blue sea at the end of the rainbow. A year from this coming June. I had to set the date so far off because I want Socrates to come, too, and if he starts tomorrow it will take him until a year or so from now to get there.

SOCRATES

It's very kind of you to think of me, Kalotté.

OFOTI

Yes, thank you very much, Kalotté. I'll mark that down on my calendar. (*Picks up hammer and chisel and moves across to rock calendar*)

KALOTTÉ

But wait, Ofoti; listen to my new idea. I want to invite this lovely human being to come too, because he really is . . . well, at least he seems to be just as nice as turtles or trolls. And so instead of having the party next year, I'll have it tomorrow. I'll carry you across the sea on my back, Ofoti, and, Socrates, you can hold onto my hair and I'll pull you along behind me. That way we won't have to wait a whole year for you.

OFOTI

But, Kalotté, how are we going to get the Boy there? He

could never swim such a distance, and even if we get a dolphin to take him, how can he enjoy your party when he'll have to hold his breath all the time he's in your house in the blue water?

KALOTTÉ

Oh, Ofoti, you're certainly right. I hadn't thought of that.

OFOTI

But don't feel bad, because I have another idea. Why not have the party right here, right now? We're all here, aren't we? and it's right now, isn't it? so what is there to stop us?

SOCRATES

Ofoti, sometimes you're almost bright enough to be a turtle.

KALOTTÉ

Oh, Ofoti. How kind of you to ask us!

BOY (*Jumping up and down*)

Hurrah, hurrah, hurrah! There's going to be a party—with a mermaid, a turtle, and a troll. And I'm invited even though I am a human being. Oh, I just knew there was a troll somewhere in the world, and I knew he didn't really eat little boys. The word troll is so lovely! Wait till I get back and tell my mother that she was wrong. And that the Troll has the most marvelous parties right in his underneath the bridge house. Oh, I'm so happy I could dance.

(*Boy breaks into dance. Ofoti, Kalotté, and Socrates join hands with Boy and they all dance to the music of the "Troll Song."*)

CURTAIN

ACT III

(Spot on Narrator on apron, stage right, with book. On dark stage there is tableau of Boy, Ofoti, Socrates, and Kalotté during the party. Ofoti has on an apron, and is carrying a garbage can lid on which are tin cans with peppermint straws in them, slices of watermelon rind, and a huge chocolate cake. Socrates sits in the pose of "The Thinker." Kalotté, in dance pose, with arms twined over her head, is standing tall, about to snap her fingers.)

NARRATOR

It was the most splendid party the Boy had ever gone to in his life. *(Curtain rises. Tableau is gradually lighted.)* Kalotté sang and danced. Socrates answered questions even before the Boy was able to think them up. Ofoti served the refreshments and was just kind and lovely. They drank seaweed juice from tin cans through "saltmint" straws—the Boy liked the flavor of saltmint even better than peppermint. They ate slices of "air melon," which you could eat and eat and eat because it didn't fill you up the way watermelon did. And there was a delicious chocolate cake which Ofoti called "human food cake," although the Boy said it tasted almost the same as what his mother called devil's food cake—but better. Then, all of a sudden, when the party was at its very gayest . . .

(Light out on Narrator, who then exits)

[51]

BOY *(Leaping in air)*
Hurrah, hurrah, hurrah! I'll do it, oh, I'll do it!

SOCRATES
(Going up to Boy and shaking his hand) Congratulations.
Aren't you going to congratulate him, Kalotté? . . . and you,
Ofoti?

OFOTI
Certainly, Socrates. But what is it he's going to do?

SOCRATES
Why, he's . . . he's . . . going to do something that deserves
congratulations, aren't you?

BOY
That's right. I've decided that I'm not going back.

OFOTI
Not going back?

SOCRATES
Not going back?

KALOTTÉ
Not going back?

BOY
No. I'm not going to go back to the world of human beings.
Instead, I'm just going to go on living underneath this bridge
with you forever, Ofoti . . . . But you don't seem glad.

SOCRATES
Of course, of course, we're glad. Why, we're just delighted.
(Looks very mournful) Nothing could make us happier. But
. . . well . . . you see. Uh . . . you tell him, Ofoti.

OFOTI
Well . . . what Socrates means is . . . that is . . . uh . . .
Kalotté, you explain it to him.

(Ofoti and Socrates turn their backs, place their hands be-

hind themselves, and hang their heads. Kalotté throws her
arms around Boy.)

KALOTTÉ

You see, what you don't understand is that . . . well, Ofoti
and I, trolls and mermaids, we're really not what people call
real. There now, that's the terrible truth.

BOY

Then my Mother was right after all. And the Rich Man and
the Wise Man, too.

KALOTTÉ

Well . . . in a way . . .

OFOTI *(Wheeling around)*

No, no, don't believe that. You were right even if we're not
really real. Because we do exist, as you can see with your
own eyes. It's just that we're really not real.

BOY

But if I were to become really not real, then couldn't I stay
with you? Look at Socrates. He's real, I know, because everyone knows that turtles are real. And he's here with you often,
so he must also be *not* real, too. I wouldn't mind being not
real, either, if I could live with you, Ofoti, underneath this
bridge.

OFOTI

Well, I don't know . . . I just don't know . . .

BOY

Say *yes*, Ofoti. Please do.

OFOTI *(Wincing)*

What do you think, Socrates?

SOCRATES

It wouldn't work. Not at all. You just can't decide that you're
going to be really *not* real, just as Ofoti and Kalotté can't
decide that they're going to be really real. A being is either

[53]

not real, like Ofoti, or real, like you, my boy, or real and not real at the same time, like me. You are what you are. You can't make yourself something else.

BOY

Oh. *(About to cry)*

OFOTI

It must be true if Socrates says so. But please don't feel bad. *(Comforts Boy)* Maybe you can find your way here again sometime. And besides, we're all really here together now, aren't we? even though some of us are really real and some of us really not real and some of us really not real and really real at the same time. Let's go on with our party.

(Kalotté has resumed dance, Ofoti is extending tray to Boy, Socrates has fallen into "The Thinker" pose. Suddenly, loud sound of Chauffeur making noise of a pneumatic drill on rock outside Ofoti's door interrupts Boy's question. Kalotté stops dancing, veils face, and runs to edge of stage left in fear. Ofoti drops tray and covers ears as he looks around in pain and terror.)

SOCRATES

The answer to the question you were just about to ask, my boy, is *now*. *(Socrates pulls head inside shell and drops onto all fours.)*

BOY

I won't answer the rock. Ever. No, I'll never leave you, Ofoti. *(Boy runs over and hugs Ofoti, who is now, along with Socrates and Kalotté, frozen.)*

(Chauffeur with drill, Rich Man flipping silver dollar, Secretary with roll of plans and Geiger counter enter. All have telephones hanging around their necks and earphones over their ears.)

BOY *(Blocking them)*

You can't come in.

[54]

SECRETARY

(Brushing Boy aside and with big steps leading the way for Rich Man's Chauffeur while talking into mouthpiece of telephone) Let's try it right here.

BOY

Get out. You aren't allowed in here.

SECRETARY

(Paying no attention to Boy) Or maybe we'd better start over here. *(Stopping right beside Ofoti, but not seeing him)*

BOY

Stop it, stop it!

SECRETARY

Are you talking to us, Boy?

BOY

Yes. You have no right just coming in. No one answered when you knocked.

SECRETARY

Knocked? We didn't knock. What in the world would we knock for?

BOY

Why, this is Ofoti's house. To walk into people's houses without being invited is impolite.

SECRETARY

We're sorry, Boy, but we haven't time to talk to you now. Look us up toward the end of next month and maybe then we can give you an appointment for sometime along in the middle of this coming summer, if the matter is really important. *(To Rich Man. All communication among Rich Man, Wise Man, the two Secretaries, and the two Chauffeurs is by way of telephone.)* We're ready to begin drilling, sir. Shall we go ahead?

RICH MAN

Hmm . . . yes . . . yes . . . go ahead.

[55]

BOY

Stop! What are you going to do?

SECRETARY

Didn't we just tell you we're busy?

BOY

But I have a right to know.

SECRETARY

Silly Boy. No one has a right to anything.

BOY

But don't you remember me? I'm the boy who caught his *(Pointing to Rich Man)* silver dollar for him when he was playing tiddleywinks.

SECRETARY
(Glancing at Boy from head to toe)

Well . . . so you are. Look, we're tearing down this bridge, Boy.

BOY

Tearing down the bridge! But it's Ofoti's home. You just can't come along and tear down a person's home. Besides, the noise would kill Ofoti and probably Socrates and Kalotté, too. No. I won't let you.

SECRETARY

Whatever are you talking about?

BOY *(Pointing)*

Ofoti, that Troll. And Kalotté, the Mermaid over there. And Socrates, this Turtle.

SECRETARY

Troll? Mermaid? We thought we settled that business with you once and for all.

BOY

Oh, you remember, do you? You remember saying there was

[56]

no such thing as a troll anywhere in the world? Well, what do you say now?

SECRETARY

The same thing—there's no such thing as a troll anywhere in the world. If Farthington, Farthington, Farthington, and Lump can't locate . . .

BOY

But look! Right there in front of you—Ofoti the Troll.

SECRETARY

What? Are you trying to make fools of us?

BOY

No, no. Just reach out your hand and you can touch him . . . and Kalotté the Mermaid, can't you see her standing over there? And here, right in front of me, Socrates the Turtle. Do you mean you can't see this Turtle?

SECRETARY

Of course we see that turtle, Boy. Do you think we're blind? Ugh. What a slimy creature! But if you think that any old turtle is going to keep us from tearing down this bridge and getting our hands on the pot of gold, so to speak . . .

BOY

Pot of gold?

SECRETARY

Pot of gold—that *is* what we said. In case you didn't know, this is the place where the rainbow ends. That pot of gold is worth half the wealth in the world. And since we already are in possession of the first half, why . . .

BOY

You're crazy if you think this is the end of the rainbow. The rainbow has its end out in the blue sea, where Kalotté the Mermaid lives. Oh, you're making a great mistake if you think . . .

SECRETARY

Nonsense, Boy. Right here is where the rainbow ends. And we can prove it. *(To Chauffeur)* Bring in the evidence.

(Chauffeur gestures offstage and Wise Man's Chauffeur enters with shiny new wheelbarrow, full of books, followed by Wise Man's Secretary and then Wise Man, now in full dress suit, with high silk hat, smoking huge cigar.)

BOY

Why, it's the Wise Man! Tell him, Wise Man, tell him that the rainbow doesn't end here and that there's no pot of gold buried underneath this bridge. You must know that, at least.

(Secretary snaps fingers at Wise Man.)

WISE MAN

Quite to the contrary, my boy. It was I who first discovered that a pot of gold, so to speak, is indeed buried under this bridge and that therefore this must be the end of the rainbow, at least metaphorically speaking. When you so thoughtlessly ran into me a little while ago, I was just completing my researches and was on my way to find someone who could put my great discovery to use. As you can see . . . ahem . . . I've come upon happier days. *(Flicks ashes from cigar with little finger)*

BOY

I don't believe it. Everything you told me before was wrong. *(To Rich Man's Secretary)* You don't really believe what he tells you, do you? He doesn't know anything at all.

WISE MAN

(Grabbing book from top of wheelbarrow and handing it to his Secretary) Read to this ignorant Boy, my good man.

WISE MAN'S SECRETARY

When the needle-like electrode detects the passage through the tube's walls of ionizing particles by the momentary current

[58]

set up on ionization of the contained gas, then *uranium* has to be present.

(Wise Man points to Geiger counter Secretary is holding and vigorously nods head up and down.)

SECRETARY

There now, do you see?

BOY

That didn't say anything about a pot of gold. It was about something called *uranium. (Secretary and Wise Man nod and smile to each other.)* Besides, there is no such thing as a pot of gold at the end of the rainbow. That's just a story that got started because someone saw the golden hair of Kalotté the Mermaid shimmering underneath the blue ocean.

SECRETARY

We can see that you're a very ill-informed boy. In this day and age every boy with the least bit of education knows that no one cares any longer about what used to be called gold. What we're after these days is power. Wise Man, explain to this Boy the value of the uranium deposit that lies underneath this bridge.

WISE MAN

(Grabbing another book, opening it at random, handing it to his Secretary) Be so kind as to read, my good man.

WISE MAN'S SECRETARY

Uranium is capable of capturing neutrons, forming an element of atomic number higher than 92. In the breakdown of such a radioactive isotope, the transuranic element precipitates a nuclear reaction.

WISE MAN

In short, whoever controls the uranium in the world can make the biggest noise.

SECRETARY

That's us—or at least it's going to be.

Noise! Why you can't add to the noise that's being made already. Not a troll or a mermaid or a turtle anywhere will be able to survive.

SECRETARY

Don't be silly, Boy. *(To Chauffeur)* When we say *uranium,* start drilling.

BOY

Wait! Do you remember that when I caught the Rich Man's silver dollar and returned it to him so he could go on with his game of tiddleywinks he told me that I could have a bridge as a reward? Well, I'll take this bridge.

(Secretary whispers to Wise Man in great consternation. Wise Man whispers to his Secretary, who begins to search through books. Then Wise Man and Rich Man's Secretary begin frenzied searching of books. Secretary looks up at Boy and smiles defensively.)

BOY

Well, give me my bridge.

SECRETARY

(Laughs ingratiatingly, then rings Rich Man on telephone) We're terribly sorry to bother you, sir, but we've run into a little problem—a boy.

RICH MAN

A boy! That's no problem.

SECRETARY

But, sir, he's the Boy you promised a bridge to as a reward for catching your silver dollar. Now he demands this bridge.

RICH MAN

Sometimes I wonder what I'm paying you and that fool of a Wise Man for. It certainly isn't brains. And people say that I'm an idiot just because I like to play tiddleywinks. As a matter of fact, I don't like to play tiddleywinks—I hate the game. The only reason I play is to make people believe that I'm stupid, whereas actually I do all the thinking. And the Wise Man and my Secretary, who seem to have all the brains —why, they're perfect fools. Listen, you idiot—let the Boy have his bridge. Do you think I would ever go back on a promise? But first tear the bridge down, then throw the pieces of rock on the other side of the river. I never promised him that the bridge would be built nor did I ever promise to give him the land underneath the bridge. And be sure to remind him that I like, no, I love people, especially boys. Now let's get drilling for that pot of uranium.

SECRETARY

Very well, sir. *(To Boy)* You may have your bridge, Boy, but we're going to move it . . .

BOY

Oh, do you think I'm deaf? Do you think I can't hear him just because I'm not listening on that telephone of yours? How awful human beings are! If only somehow I could get Ofoti and Socrates and Kalotté away from these terrible people . . . if only the Mars Man . . . *(Grabs Secretary's telephone)* Please, Mars Man, come down and help . . .

RICH MAN *(Answering telephone)*

What's that? Don't you know you aren't permitted to talk to me without an appoint . . .

BOY

I hate you, Rich Man. I think you're the meanest human being in the whole world. And I don't believe that you love or even like people, especially boys.

RICH MAN

Oh, but I do—when they don't get in my way. Idiot, get that Boy off this telephone. *(Secretary grabs telephone from Boy.)* Now in exactly sixty seconds we start drilling. *(Pulls out gold watch and addresses Secretary)* Let me know when sixty seconds is up.

SECRETARY *(To Wise Man)*

Let us know when sixty seconds is up.

WISE MAN *(To his Secretary)*

Let me know when sixty seconds is up, my good man.

(Wise Man's Chauffeur, Wise Man's Secretary, Wise Man, Rich Man, Rich Man's Secretary all cluster around Rich Man's outstretched hand with watch. Rich Man raises other hand as a signal; Rich Man's Chauffeur with hands on drill waits for signal. Mars Man descends in trash can with a gentle swoosh. Rich Man, Wise Man, etc. freeze. Ofoti, Socrates, and Kalotté come to life.)

BOY

Oh, Mars Man, you heard me and you came!

MARS MAN

Of course. Didn't I tell you I'd come whenever you called?

BOY

I'm so glad, because a terrible thing is about to . . .

SOCRATES

Excuse me, my boy, but I must say good-bye. *(To Ofoti)* It really was a lovely party, Ofoti, while it lasted, and I hate to be crawling off like this.

MARS MAN

Don't be afraid, Socrates, you needn't hurry.

SOCRATES

Afraid? Who said anything about hurrying? . . . It's just . . . Well, it's just that I can't stomach noise and those crazy human beings are about ready to . . .

MARS MAN

Oh, don't concern yourself about them. As long as I'm here they can't even move.

[62]

BOY

Is that true, Mars Man? Hurrah, hurrah, hurrah!

MARS MAN

Yes, it's true. You see, in the Lovely Silence there really is no such thing as passing time and when I come down to Earth I bring a little world of timelessness with me. Until the instant I depart, people who are in time but not in my little timeless world can't move on to the next second.

BOY, OFOTI, SOCRATES, KALOTTÉ

Ahhh!

BOY

Well, while we have time . . . I mean as long as we have no time . . . I'd like to introduce you to Kalotté the Mermaid, Socrates the Turtle, and Ofoti the Troll. Do you remember, Mars Man, that I asked you whether or not there was such a being as a troll in Space the last time you were down? Well, I found the troll right here on Earth. All the people who told me there was no such being were wrong.

MARS MAN

I know. I found out all about trolls, too. I thought up the idea "troll" in the *Thoughtopedia* and what do you think I discovered?

BOY

What?

MARS MAN

That trolls are not Earth beings at all. They belong to the Lovely Silence just like me. They come from that part of Space that you Earth creatures call the Constellation Ursa Major or the Great Bear. They're really very beautiful beings.

BOY

You mean trolls come from nowhere on Earth?

MARS MAN

That's right. Ofoti and the other Earth trolls are descended

[63]

from two Heavenly trolls who slid down the rainbow for
fun one day and couldn't get back up.

BOY

(Grabbing Socrates and dancing with him) Hurrah, hurrah,
hurrah! You answered the question correctly after all, Socrates.
Don't you remember, you said that the answer to where trolls
came from was, nowhere in the world? Why you're even
wiser than you know.

SOCRATES

Ha, ha, ha. Wait till I tell my cousin Alcibiades. Won't he
stand up in his shell and take notice.

BOY

But the reason I called you, Mars Man, is Kalotté and Socrates
and Ofoti. When you leave and time starts moving again, the
Rich Man is going to begin drilling right here, so that he
can get something called uranium, which he says can make
an even louder noise than the drilling. My friends will never
be able to stand it. They'll all die. Unless . . .

SOCRATES

Don't worry about me, my boy. If I can get back into the
water, I'll drown out most of their racket and I swear I'll
never leave the lovely gurgle of the ocean again.

KALOTTÉ

And don't worry about me, sweet Boy. I can return to my
home in the blue sea at the end of the rainbow and go on
with my singing. It's Ofoti who is in great danger.

SOCRATES

Correct. He won't even have a bridge over his head.

OFOTI

Please don't be concerned about me. You can see that there's
no longer any use for me on Earth. Every hundred years it
gets harder and harder for me to find a human being to

[64]

believe in me so that I can go on living. And of course now I know that I don't really belong here anyway. The rest of you must leave before they begin their noise-making—Socrates and Kalotté into the blue sea, Mars Man back into the Lovely Silence, and you, dear Boy, back to the world of only real things. I truly believe it's time for me to die.

BOY

(Running to Ofoti and clutching him) Oh no, Ofoti, you mustn't say that. Mars Man, the reason I called you is to ask whether you'd take Ofoti with you in your imagination ship. I thought he might be able to live with you on Mars, but since it turns out that trolls really come from the Great Bear, why, perhaps you can return him to his own people.

MARS MAN

I'll be glad to. I'm sure that the Troll People—"the Beautiful Ones" we space men think of them as—will be happy to see you, Ofoti, and to learn all about your strange life down here. Everyone in the Lovely Silence has heard what a curious place Earth is.

OFOTI

If you're sure I won't be putting you to any trouble . . .

BOY

Hurrah, hurrah, hurrah! Ofoti is going back to his people.

KALOTTÉ

To be in the Lovely Silence.

SOCRATES

To live among the Beautiful Ones.

BOY

I'm so happy . . . *(Starts to cry)* But . . .
(Kalotté throws her arms around Boy.)

MARS MAN

But what?

[65]

BOY

It's just . . . just . . . *(To Ofoti)* it's just that I'll never see you again, Ofoti—ever. *(To Mars Man)* Oh, can't I go along with him? Please?

MARS MAN

Of course you *can*. It's really very easy. You must remember, though, that if you go you won't be lying in your bed tomorrow morning when your Mother comes to wake you up.

BOY

I . . . I won't?

MARS MAN

No, Earth Boy, you won't.

BOY

But Ofoti is so . . . and after getting to know him, how can I go back to the world of the Rich Man and the Wise Man and their Secretaries and Chauffeurs?

MARS MAN

You're right. It will be hard. But you know, if you do go back, you don't have to be like them. Because you'll be taking back with you something of Kalotté and Socrates and Ofoti.

BOY

Oh, I'll never forget them, no matter what.

OFOTI

And I'll always remember you too, dear Boy. I'll think about you down through the stars.

MARS MAN

Why, you can do much better than that. You can see and hear the Boy on Earth, Ofoti, whenever you want.

OFOTI

I can, Mars Man?

SOCRATES

How will Ofoti be able to see and hear the Boy through all that space, Mars Man? I'm wise but I don't understand.

MARS MAN

Of course, you don't understand, Socrates, because it's unearthly wisdom. This is how it works. Whenever anyone on Earth thinks about any being who is *not* on Earth, the unearthly being is able to see and hear the person thinking about him. That's why trolls have always had to have someone to believe in them in order to stay alive. It's the way of things in the Lovely Silence. In Earth language you call it Faith.

BOY

Gosh, is that what Faith means?

MARS MAN

Indeed it is, Earth Boy.

BOY

And you mean that if I don't go back, there won't be anyone on Earth to believe in Ofoti? That he will die after all?

MARS MAN

I'm afraid that's the way of it. Now Socrates and Kalotté, into the water—quickly. I can't hold time much longer and the Earth Boy must make his choice. Hurry, hurry! I won't leave until you're safe.

KALOTTÉ

Good-bye, sweet Boy. Thank you for listening to my song.

BOY

Good-bye, Kalotté. I'll always remember.

SOCRATES

Good-bye, my boy. I'll tell my cousin Alcibiades all about you.

BOY

Good-bye, Socrates. It was awfully nice to get to know you.

[67]

MARS MAN

Hurry! Hurry! Time is pressing, reality is pulling. The choice is yours, Earth Boy. Which will it be?

(Exit Socrates and Kalotté.)

BOY

Oh, Ofoti dear, I can't let you die. If there must be somebody in the real world to do the believing, then I'll go back. And I'll think of you all the time. I'll never let you out of my mind. Even when I'm asleep I'll dream of you. Please listen to me and see me.

OFOTI

I will, dear Boy, I will. And someday maybe . . .

MARS MAN

Only the Beautiful, only the Lovely. Swoosh . . .

(Rich Man's raised hand comes down as trash can rises and Rich Man's Chauffeur makes drilling noise and starts to drill. Rich Man and Wise Man and Secretaries shout. Boy stands horrified, then claps his hands over his ears and buries his face in his chest. Blackout.)

CURTAIN

EPILOGUE

(Boy and Harlequin are back inside tree stump house, as at the end of Act I. Boy is sitting on paint can; Harlequin is pointing with giant paint brush at picture of troll underneath a bridge he has just drawn on screen. Spot of light on Narrator on apron. As curtain rises, stage is gradually lighted dim green.)

NARRATOR

And so time commenced running again, and all of a sudden the Boy found himself back inside the tree stump house with the funny little man. A tear rolled over the edge of the Boy's eye and slithered down his cheek. Then the funny little man *(Harlequin and Boy pantomime.)* took the picture he had drawn of Ofoti underneath his bridge and he rolled it up and gave it to the Boy, explaining in his own wordless language that the Boy must keep the image of the Troll, always.

BOY

Oh, I will keep it, I will, and I'll look at Ofoti often so that I'll never forget him and he'll always be able to see me.

NARRATOR

And the funny little man went on to explain that the Boy must never show the picture to anyone, not even his parents.

BOY

I promise. I'll never show it to anyone as long as I live.

And now the moon was down from the sky and the sun was lighting out the stars.

(Boy gets up and wipes his eyes. Harlequin commences comic dance to cheer him up, but dance lacks conviction. Flat of front of tree stump house passes from right to left back over Boy and Harlequin, who are now beside the rock. Boy walks on and gradually Harlequin stops clowning and loses vigor, like a mechanical toy running down, then sits on rock in dejection. Finally Harlequin curls up in a little ball, and rock with Harlequin on it is rolled offstage. Bed and window are slid on upstage.)

NARRATOR

Looking up at the fading sparks of light in the direction of the Great Bear, the Boy walked back along the road, down and up the hills, over the bridges, and across the rivers, until he came to his own house beside the hickory tree in his own yard. *(Boy pantomimes.)* Softly he shinnied back up the rainspout, crawled in through the open window, and climbed into his bed. No sooner had he laid his head on his pillow and snuggled down underneath the covers than his Mother *(Enter Mother, pantomiming.)* entered his room and pulled up the shade. As the golden light of the morning sun came flooding in, the Boy bolted up in bed. *(Bright light on stage)* Immediately he began to tell his Mother the story of Ofoti the Troll and the Mars Man and Kalotté the Mermaid and Socrates the Turtle and the Wise Man and the Rich Man and the Secretaries and Chauffeurs and the funny little man whose name he didn't know and whom he couldn't quite explain in a proper way. His Mother listened and smiled. And when the Boy had finished the whole marvelous story, she ran her hand through his tangled hair, shook her head and smiled again, and kissed him. The Boy knew that that meant she loved him but that she didn't believe the story of Ofoti the Troll had really happened;

she believed that he had dreamed it. And then the Boy's mother told him that he must hurry and dress so that he wouldn't be late for school, and she left to make his breakfast of orange juice and oatmeal with cream and buttered toast. *(Exit Mother.)* For a moment the Boy just went on sitting in his bed. Looking through the window at the hickory tree outside, he wondered whether his mother might really be right, whether he had only dreamed of finding the Troll. Then he yawned, and stretched his arms, and the next second he threw back the covers and hopped out of bed. And there . . . right in the very spot where he had been lying and the outline of his body still was lightly drawn on the white sheet . . . there was the picture of Ofoti underneath his bridge, just as the funny little man had made it. Only the paper and the picture were much smaller than they had seemed last night, small enough for the Boy to carry in the pocket of his trousers, so that whenever he liked, without anyone's knowing it, not even his Mother, he might pull out the picture and see once again the Troll he had searched for and found.

(Black out Narrator, who then exits. Boy walks over to window and looks out as Rich Man, Secretary, Chauffeur, Wise Man, Wise Man's Secretary, Wise Man's Chauffeur, Mars Man, Socrates, Kalotté, and Ofoti, all in front of Harlequin, dancing and waving his big paint brush, sing the "Troll Song" as they parade back on stage in the sunlight.)

CURTAIN

TROLL SONG

A troll is a ter-ri-ble, ter-ri-ble thing

With a hid-e-ous, hor-ri-ble sting;

How he en-joys to gnaw on boys;

A crea-ture bold — that's a troll!

MERMAID SONG

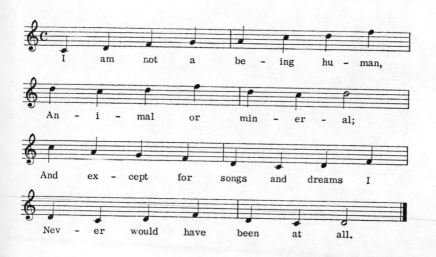

I am not a being human,
An - i - mal or min - er - al;
And ex - cept for songs and dreams I
Nev - er would have been at all.

Date Due